Oceans, Seas, and Coasts

By Jan Anderson

Contents

Introduction

Oceans and seas cover most of Earth. They are large areas of salty water.

Oceans and seas are important to us in different ways.

Pacific Ocean

DID YOU KNOW?

The Pacific Ocean is the biggest ocean on Earth.

We get fish and other foods from the sea.

Ships sail across the oceans,
carrying heavy cargoes of food and other goods
from one country to another.

Oceans

Oceans are shallow near land,
and very deep further out.
It is cold and dark
in the deepest parts of the ocean.

Some oceans have colourful reefs
where many different fish live.

The bottom of the ocean is not flat.
In some places there are deep trenches.

The Mariana Trench is the deepest trench of all.
It is in the Pacific Ocean.

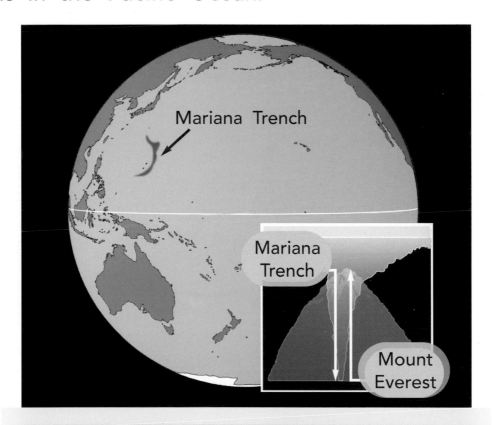

Mariana Trench

Mariana Trench

Mount Everest

DID YOU KNOW?

The depth of the Mariana Trench is almost the same as the height of Mount Everest.

Seas

Seas are not as big, or as deep, as oceans.
There is more land around seas
than around oceans.

Many seas open into an ocean.

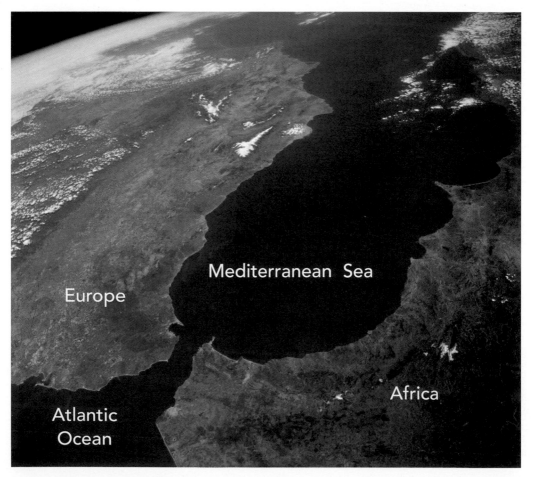

Mediterranean Sea

Europe

Atlantic
Ocean

Africa

The Dead Sea is an inland sea.
It is called the Dead Sea
because almost nothing can live in it.

It is so salty that most things can float in it.

Seafood

We eat many kinds of fish
from the seas and oceans.

There are many types of seafood that people like to eat, including shellfish and some small sea animals.

In some countries, people eat seaweed that has been dried.

Islands

An island is an area of land
in the middle of water.
There are thousands of islands
in the world.
Some islands are very big.
Other islands are so tiny
that nobody lives on them.

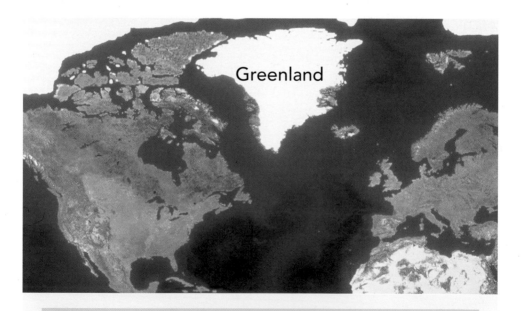

Greenland

DID YOU KNOW?

The biggest island in the world is Greenland.

There are coral islands
in some parts of the world.

Some islands were made by volcanoes
under the sea.

The Coast

The coast is where the land meets the sea.
Many coasts have beaches
that are covered in sand or small stones.

In some places, there are high cliffs
along the coast.

These cliffs were made by huge waves
crashing against the land.

Many years ago,
glaciers cut deep valleys into the coast
in some parts of the world.
These valleys were filled by the sea.
Deep valleys of water are called fiords.

DID YOU KNOW?

Some fiords are deep enough
for big ships to sail in.

Sometimes, people leave garbage
on the beach or throw it into the sea.
The garbage can kill sea animals.

DID YOU KNOW?

Sea animals can die
when they get caught
in plastic.

Ships sometimes spill oil into the sea.

BIG OIL SPILL

An oil tanker has spilled its cargo. Rocks and beaches along the coast are covered in oil.

People from nearby towns are working day and night to save the seabirds. The birds cannot swim or fly because their feathers are covered with oil.

It's going to be months before the beaches are clean again.

Lighthouses

Lighthouses have been built
along many coasts.
They have strong lights
to warn ships
about dangerous rocks and the coastline.

Machines turn on the lights after dark.

Many ships were wrecked off rocky coasts
before lighthouses were built.

Shipwreck Survivor's Story

The night was long as I held onto the wreck
of our ship. I thought that morning would
never come.

Big waves washed over me. I kept hoping
that someone on the coast would see
the wreck in the water and rescue me!

It was so cold that my hands could hardly
move. Pieces of ship were floating around me.
Other people were crying out for help.

However, we were very lucky.
People on the coast had seen us.
They used boats to rescue us.

Andrew Ryan
July 4, 1845
near the coast of Australia

The Changing Coastline

The shape of the coast is called the coastline.

Over hundreds of years, coastlines can change.
Big storms and strong waves
crash against the coast.
The waves wash the soil away.

After a big storm,
the sea flooded this town on the coast.

In some places,
people have changed the coastline.
They have made land out of the sea.

First they built strong walls in the sea,
then they used windmills
to pump out the sea water.

Now there are flower farms
on some of this new land.

People and the Sea

We use the ocean for many things.
Ships use it to carry cargo.
People who fish use it to bring seafood
into our markets and stores.

We walk along the coast
and have picnics on the beach.
We use the sea for swimming and sailing.

Questions

1. What is the biggest ocean on Earth?
2. What is the deepest trench in the ocean?
3. What is the biggest island in the world?
4. How do we know that some fiords are very big?
5. What can happen when sea animals get caught in plastic?

Glossary

coral	something that is hard and is made by tiny sea creatures
fiord	one kind of place where the sea flows in between high cliffs
glacier	a river of ice
inland	land that is away from the sea
trench	deep valley on the ocean floor
volcano (volcanoes)	a mountain that is formed when liquid rock breaks through the surface of Earth